What's So Great About . . . ?

HARRIET TUBMAN

Amie Jane Leavitt

Mitchell Lane
PUBLISHERS

P.O. Box 196
Hockessin, Delaware 19707
Visit us on the web: www.mitchelllane.com
Comments? email us: mitchelllane@mitchelllane.com

Mitchell Lane PUBLISHERS

Printing   1   2   3   4   5   6   7   8   9

A Robbie Reader/What's So Great About . . . ?

Amelia Earhart	Anne Frank	Annie Oakley
Christopher Columbus	Daniel Boone	Davy Crockett
Elizabeth Blackwell	Ferdinand Magellan	Francis Scott Key
Galileo	George Washington Carver	**Harriet Tubman**
Helen Keller	Henry Hudson	Jacques Cartier
Johnny Appleseed	Paul Bunyan	Robert Fulton
Rosa Parks	Sam Houston	

Library of Congress Cataloging-in-Publication Data
Leavitt, Amie Jane.
    Harriet Tubman / by Amie Jane Leavitt.
        p. cm. — (A Robbie reader. What's so great about — ?)
    Includes bibliographical references and index.
    Audience: Grades K-3.
    ISBN 978-1-58415-577-5 (library bound)
    1. Tubman, Harriet, 1820?–1913 — Juvenile literature. 2. Slaves — United States — Biography — Juvenile literature. 3. African American women — Biography — Juvenile literature. 4. Underground railroad — Juvenile literature. I. Title.
E444.T82L43 2008
973.7'115092 — dc22
[B]
                                                                        2007000822

ABOUT THE AUTHOR: Amie Jane Leavitt is the author of numerous articles, puzzles, workbooks, and tests for kids and teens. She is a former teacher who has taught all subjects and grade levels. Ms. Leavitt loves to travel, play tennis, and learn new things everyday as she writes. She, too, believes in following your dreams.

PHOTO CREDITS: Cover, p. 12 — North Wind Picture Archives; pp. 1, 3, 8 — Hulton Archive/Getty Images; p. 6 — *Bound For the Promised Land: Harriet Tubman, Portrait of an American Hero* by Kate Clifford Lawson/Map by Bill Wilson; p. 14 — The Granger Collection, New York; p. 16 — Bryson Bernada/ Library of Congress; pp. 18, 22, 26 — Library of Congress; p. 19 — James and Susan Meredith; p. 20 — *The Underground Railroad*/Raymond Bial; p. 21 — MPI/Getty Images; p. 25 — National Park Service.

PUBLISHER'S NOTE: The following story has been thoroughly researched and to the best of our knowledge represents a true story. While every possible effort has been made to ensure accuracy, the publisher will not assume liability for damages caused by inaccuracies in the data, and makes no warranty on the accuracy of the information contained herein.

                                                                        PPC

TABLE OF CONTENTS

Words in **bold** type can be found in the glossary.

HARRIET TUBMAN
A PASSAGE TO FREEDOM

Harriet Tubman leads slaves to freedom on the Underground Railroad. In 1868, Frederick Douglass wrote in a letter to Harriet: "The midnight sky and the silent stars have been the witnesses of your devotion to freedom and of your heroism."

Running to Freedom

Harriet ran as fast as she could through the dark night. The sky was filled with stars. She looked for that special star her father had shown her when she was a child. It was called the North Star. It would help her find her way to the free states in the North.

When Harriet grew tired, she stopped at houses that she knew were safe. The people who lived in them were part of the Underground Railroad. This railroad wasn't a train, and it wasn't under the ground. It was a secret network of trails and people who helped slaves escape to freedom.

It took Harriet many days to travel from her home in Maryland to the safety of the

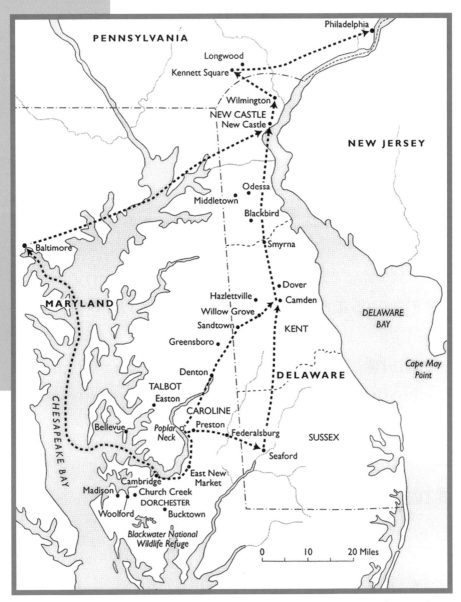

Harriet followed many different routes out of Maryland and into the freedom of the North. She was careful to follow different routes all the time. This prevented the trackers from finding her.

North. Finally, she made it to Pennsylvania (pen-sul-VAYN-yuh). When Harriet knew she was free, she looked down at her hands. She expected them to look different, but she was still the same Harriet. Yet somehow she felt a little different. She had just made a very brave trip through forests and streams, avoiding towns and trackers. She was finally free.

Harriet felt like a strange person in a strange land. She felt like a visitor. Her home was with her family, and her family was still in slavery in the South.

Right then, Harriet made an important decision. She would return to the South to get her family. It would be dangerous. If she were caught, she would no longer be free—and she might even be killed. But she knew that she would never feel truly free inside until her family was free, too.

Harriet talked about the day she crossed the line into the North and freedom. "I looked at my hands," she said, "to see if I was the same person now I was free."

Minty

Harriet Araminta (ayr-uh-MIN-tuh) Ross was born in 1821 on the Eastern Shore of Maryland. The exact date is not known, and some sources give the year of her birth as 1819 or 1820. Harriet was born on a **plantation** (plan-TAY-shun) owned by Edward Brodas (BROH-duhs), which is sometimes spelled *Brodess*. Her parents, Harriet Green and Benjamin Ross, were both slaves. Children of slaves, including Harriet, were automatically slaves, too.

Since her mother's name was Harriet, people called little Harriet "Minty." Minty had ten brothers and sisters.

As a young child, Minty would sometimes play in the woods with her brothers and sisters. She loved running through the orchards and smelling the peaches, pears, and apples growing on the trees. Harriet was not allowed to eat this fruit, so she would just breathe deeply to enjoy the wonderful scent. Slaves were not allowed to have such nice things.

Harriet's family lived in a tiny wooden shack. It had one room, a door, a roof, and walls but no windows. Everyone slept on the dirt floor.

Minty's childhood was very short, because slave children began working at a young age. When Minty was just six years old, Master Brodas hired her to the Cook family. She had to leave her own family and help the Cooks with chores in their house. She took care of their baby all night. Even in the pouring rain, she worked outside doing farm chores. Since she was so young, Minty didn't know how to do all the things that they asked her to do. No one had showed her how. When she made mistakes, the Cooks would get angry and lash her with a whip.

Before long, Minty became very sick, and the Cooks sent her home. Minty's mother nursed her back to health. As soon as she was well again, Master Brodas sent her off to work for another family.

Every family seemed to be as mean as the last. One time, when Minty was seven, she saw some sugar in a bowl on the table. She had never had sugar before, so she reached up to try some. The master's wife saw her. She grabbed the whip and started to chase Minty.

Minty ran far away from the plantation. She hid in a pig pen for five days and ate potato scraps with the animals. Finally, nearly starving, she came out and took the **punishment** (PUH-nish-ment) she knew was coming to her. She was whipped until her back bled.

Harriet must have been scared when she ran away from her master's plantation. She probably felt the same way every time she helped another group of slaves to freedom. Yet she knew that she must be free. She said, "There was one of two things that I had a *right* to, liberty or death. . . . I should fight for my liberty as long as my strength lasted."

Minty Becomes Harriet

Hard times continued for Minty. She wasn't alone. Many slaves were mistreated by their masters. Once, Minty wouldn't help catch a slave who was running away. The angry overseer threw a two-pound weight at the runaway. It hit Minty instead. She fell to the ground and almost died. She had a huge scar on her face for the rest of her life.

The other slaves thought Harriet was brave to stand up to the overseer. They didn't think of her as a child anymore, so they no longer called her Minty. She was now called Harriet.

When Harriet was twenty-three, she married John Tubman. He was an African American like Harriet, but he was not a slave.

Nat Turner led a slave rebellion in Virginia in 1831. Many people were killed in this uprising. It led to stricter laws against African Americans, both free and slave, in the state of Virginia.

His parents had been freed by their master, so John had been born free.

Harriet wanted to be free more than anything. She dreamed about it often. She heard about Nat Turner, a slave who had tried to help other slaves escape to freedom. The plantation owners became angry, and Nat Turner was killed.

Harriet thought Nat Turner was a brave man. She wanted to try to gain her freedom like he did. She told John about her dream, but he said she was crazy. She would never be able to get away. They would catch her and bring her back, and then he might get into trouble, too. John told Harriet that if she kept talking about running away, he would tell her master. This hurt Harriet. She didn't want her own husband to **betray** (bee-TRAY) her, so she never talked to him about it again.

Bernarda Bryson painted Harriet Tubman kneeling in prayer. Harriet was a very religious person. She didn't just say her morning and evening prayers, but, whenever she felt a need, she said, she "simply told God of it, and trusted him to set the matter right."

Moses for Her People

One day, Harriet heard about a change on the plantation. Her master was going to sell her and some of her brothers to a chain gang. They would be locked in chains and marched to another state. Harriet was afraid. Many slaves were sold, and they never saw their families again. She didn't want this to happen to her.

Harriet and her brothers decided to run away together. One night when John was asleep, Harriet slipped out the door. All she took with her was a small sack of food.

She and her brothers had gone only a little way when her brothers grew frightened. They were so afraid of getting caught, they decided

In a chain gang, the prisoners were chained together by their ankles and forced to march across many miles. Then they were forced to work for hours and hours without a break. If anyone stopped working or fell down in the march, all of the people in the chain gang could be whipped. Harriet and her brothers fled before they were sold to a chain gang.

to go back. Harriet did not. She told them she would keep going.

After Harriet reached freedom in Pennsylvania, she became a **conductor** (kun-DUK-ter) on the Underground Railroad. Conductors helped other slaves follow the path to freedom. She helped bring most of her

When Harriet and her brothers ran away, Eliza Brodas (spelled *Brodess* in this ad) offered a reward for their capture and return.

THREE HUNDRED DOLLARS REWARD.

RANAWAY from the subscriber on Monday the 17th ult., three negroes, named as follows: HARRY, aged about 19 years, has on one side of his neck a wen, just under the ear, he is of a dark chestnut color, about 5 feet 8 or 9 inches hight; BEN, aged aged about 25 years, is very quick to speak when spoken to, he is of a chestnut color, about six feet high; MINTY, aged about 27 years, is of a chestnut color, fine looking, and about 5 feet high. One hundred dollars reward will be given for each of the above named negroes, if taken out of the State, and $50 each if taken in the State. They must be lodged in Baltimore, Easton or Cambridge Jail, in Maryland.

ELIZA ANN BRODESS,
Near Bucktown, Dorchester county, Md.
Oct. 3d, 1849.

☞The Delaware Gazette will please copy the above three weeks, and charge this office.

family to the North. She even brought her parents in a wagon, since they were too old to walk. It must have been extra hard to drive that wagon through the woods and not get caught.

Harriet traveled the Underground Railroad nineteen times. She helped over 300 people become free, and she never lost one passenger. Conducting was a very dangerous job. Sometimes Harriet dressed in **disguises** (dis-GUY-ses). She would dress like a man, or

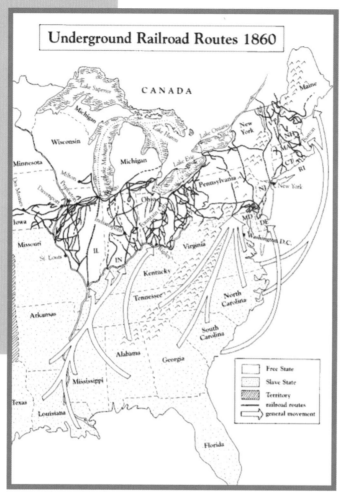

Underground Railroad Routes 1860

The Underground Railroad stretched from the Deep South in Louisiana all the way to Canada. Along the way, the runaway slaves would hide in "stations" belonging to people who disagreed with slavery. Slaves would hide in barns, attics, cellars, closets, or even underneath beds.

she would wear a fancy scarf to look like a rich lady. If she were caught, she would probably have been killed, just as Nat Turner was.

Harriet wasn't afraid, though. She was a religious person. She believed God was on her side and He would help her. Harriet became

Harriet Tubman and her family, from left to right: Harriet, her adopted daughter Gertie Davis, Harriet's husband Nelson Davis, Harriet's great-great-niece Lee Cheney, "Pop" (John) Alexander, Walter Green, "Blind Aunty" Sarah Parker, and Harriet's great-niece Dora Stewart.

known as the Moses of her people. Moses was a prophet from the Bible. He helped the Israelites (IS-reel-yts) escape slavery in Egypt (EE-jupt). Harriet was doing the same thing for slaves in America.

Not everyone liked Harriet. The plantation owners in the South were very angry with her for taking their slaves away. They offered a $40,000 reward for her capture.

Slaves in the South dreamed of one day becoming free. Harriet Tubman made that dream come true for many of them. She helped hundreds of slaves escape to freedom on the Underground Railroad.

General Tubman

In 1861, when Harriet was about forty years old, the Civil War started. The Union Army was in the North. They asked Harriet to help them as they fought the Confederate (kun-FEH-der-it) Army in the South. At first, she worked as a nurse. Then they asked her to help them by spying on the South. She knew the trails between the North and South better than anyone. One time, she helped capture a whole camp of Southern soldiers. The North called her General Tubman because of what she did for the Union.

After the war, Harriet moved to New York. She wanted to help former slaves, so she opened a house for people who had nowhere else to live.

Harriet Tubman once lived in this house on South Street in Fleming, New York. She allowed the homeless, sick, and poor to stay with her. In 1903, she gave the house to the African Methodist Episcopal Zion Church.

Harriet also started helping with the women's rights movement. She believed that everyone should have the same freedoms. She thought that women and men should have the same rights. After all, she had done the same work as men all her life. She had carried

Harriet Tubman served others all her life. On her tombstone reads the inscription: "Servant of God, Well Done."

Harriet Tubman Day, 1990

By the President of the United States of America

A Proclamation

In celebrating Harriet Tubman's life, we remember her commitment to freedom and rededicate ourselves to the timeless principles she struggled to uphold. Her story is one of extraordinary courage and effectiveness in the movement to abolish slavery and to advance the noble ideals enshrined in our Nation's Declaration of Independence: "We hold these truths to be self-evident, that all men are created equal, that they are endowed by their Creator with certain unalienable Rights, that among these are Life, Liberty and the pursuit of Happiness."

After escaping from slavery herself in 1849, Harriet Tubman led hundreds of slaves to freedom by making a reported 19 trips through the network of hiding places known as the Underground Railroad. For her efforts to help ensure that our Nation always honors its promise of liberty and opportunity for all, she became known as the "Moses of her People."

Serving as a nurse, scout, cook, and spy for the Union Army during the Civil War, Harriet Tubman often risked her own freedom and safety to protect that of others. After the war, she continued working for justice and for the cause of human dignity. Today we are deeply thankful for the efforts of this brave and selfless woman—they have been a source of inspiration to generations of Americans.

In recognition of Harriet Tubman's special place in the hearts of all who cherish freedom, the Congress has passed Senate Joint Resolution 257 in observance of "Harriet Tubman Day," March 10, 1990, the 77th anniversary of her death.

NOW, THEREFORE, I, GEORGE BUSH, President of the United States of America, do hereby proclaim March 10, 1990, as Harriet Tubman Day, and I call upon the people of the United States to observe this day with appropriate ceremonies and activities.

IN WITNESS WHEREOF, I have hereunto set my hand this ninth day of March, in the year of our Lord nineteen hundred and ninety, and of the Independence of the United States of America the two hundred and fourteenth.

George Bush

George H.W. Bush proclaimed March 10, 1990, to be Harriet Tubman Day. She had died on March 10, 1913.

wood and worked in the fields. She had crept through forests, sneaking slaves to freedom. She had helped soldiers in the army. She had proved that women could do anything if they really wanted to.

During the war, Harriet met a former slave named Nelson Davis. The two fell in love and were married in 1869. Nelson and Harriet were married for nineteen years—until Nelson died in 1888.

Harriet Tubman lived a long life. On March 10, 1913, she died of **pneumonia** (noo-MOHN-yuh). She was ninety-three years old. She had done many things that others were too afraid to do. She risked her life many times so that others might live in freedom. Even today, people are inspired to live better lives because of her example.

CHRONOLOGY

1821	Harriet Araminta Ross is born in Bucktown, Maryland.
1827	She is hired out to work for the Cook family.
1834	She gets in the way of a two-pound weight aimed at another slave and is hit on the head; it leaves a scar on her forehead.
1844	She marries John Tubman, a free man.
1849	Harriet escapes to freedom on the Underground Railroad.
1850	She becomes a conductor on the Underground Railroad, risking her life to help family and strangers to freedom.
1857	She helps her parents escape to freedom.
1859	She buys a home in New York with seven acres of land from William W. Seward. He would later become President Lincoln's Secretary of State.
1860	She makes her final trip to the South to help slaves escape.
1861	When the Civil War starts, she works as a nurse for the Union Army.
1863	She begins working as a spy for the Union Army and helps capture an entire camp of Southern soldiers.
1865	She is hired to provide nursing service to wounded soldiers at Fortress Monroe in Hampton, Virginia. On her way back home to New York, she is thrown from a train by a racist conductor and is severely injured.
1867	John Tubman dies.
1869	Harriet's biography, *Scenes in the Life of Harriet Tubman*, is published; she marries Nelson Davis.
1886	*Harriet Tubman: The Moses of Her People* is published.
1888	Nelson Davis dies.
1903	Harriet gives her house to the African Methodist Episcopal Zion Church to be used to help those in need.
1913	Harriet dies of pneumonia in Auburn, New York, on March 10. She is buried with military honors.
1944	The Liberty ship *Harriet Tubman* is christened by Eleanor Roosevelt.
1994	Freedom Park is opened in Auburn, New York, as a tribute to Harriet Tubman.
1995	The U.S. government issues a postage stamp bearing Tubman's name and picture.

TIMELINE IN HISTORY

1619   First black slave in the original thirteen American colonies arrives in Virginia.

1850   The Fugitive Slave Law is passed. It requires citizens to return runaway slaves to their owners.

1857   In the Dred Scott decision, the U.S. Supreme Court rules that no slave can be a U.S. citizen.

1861   U.S. Civil War begins.

1863   President Abraham Lincoln's Emancipation Proclamation frees the slaves in rebellious states.

1864   Sojourner Truth, a former slave and a speaker against slavery, works at a government refugee camp for freed slaves in Virginia; she meets President Abraham Lincoln.

1865   President Abraham Lincoln is assassinated; the Civil War ends.

1896   U.S. Supreme Court rules that segregation in public places is legal.

1900   Booker T. Washington founds the National Negro Business League in Tuskegee, Alabama.

1920   The Nineteenth Amendment passes, granting U.S. women the right to vote.

1940   Tuskegee Institute begins training 1,000 black pilots, who will become America's first black military airmen.

1948   President Harry S Truman officially integrates the U.S. armed forces.

1954   U.S. Supreme Court rules that segregation in schools is illegal.

1955   Rosa Parks, an African American woman in Alabama, refuses to give up her seat on a city bus. This event sparks the Montgomery Bus Boycott.

1963   Martin Luther King Jr. delivers his "I have a dream" speech.

1998   U.S. Congress passes the Hate Crimes Prevention Act of 1998.

2001   Colin Powell becomes the first African American in U.S. history to hold the office of secretary of state.

2005   Condoleezza Rice becomes the first African American female to hold the office of secretary of state.

2007   The U.S. House of Representatives passes the Local Law Enforcement Hate Crimes Prevention Act. This further protects all people from acts of hate crimes.

FIND OUT MORE

Books

Gosda, Randy T. *Harriet Tubman*. Edina, Minnesota: ABDO
    Publishing Company, 2002.

McDonough, Yona Zeldis. *Who Was Harriet Tubman?* New
    York: Grosset & Dunlap, 2002.

McMullan, Kate. *The Story of Harriet Tubman: Conductor of the
    Underground Railroad*. Milwaukee, Wisconsin: Gareth
    Stevens Publishing, 1997.

Skelton, Renee. *Harriet Tubman: A Woman of Courage*. New
    York: Time, Inc., 2005.

Weatherford, Carole Boston. *Moses: When Harriet Tubman Led
    Her People to Freedom*. New York: Jump At the Sun/
    Hyperion Books for Children, 2006.

Works Consulted

Conrad, Earl. *Harriet Tubman*. Washington, D.C.: Associated
    Publishers, Inc., 1943.

Bradford, Sarah H. *Scenes in the Life of Harriet Tubman*.
    Auburn, New York: W. J. Moses, 1869.

Humez, Jean M. *Harriet Tubman: The Life and the Life Stories*.
    Madison: The University of Wisconsin Press, 2003.

Larson, Kate Clifford. *Bound for the Promised Land: Harriet
    Tubman, Portrait of an American Hero*. New York: Random
    House, 2004.

On the Internet

Harriet Tubman http://www.harriettubman.com

The Library of Congress: *Meet Amazing Americans*, "Harriet
    Tubman" http://www.americaslibrary.gov/cgi-bin/page.cgi/
    aa/tubman

New York History Net: *The Harriet Tubman Home*, "The Life of
Harriet Tubman" http://www.nyhistory.com/harriettubman/
life.htm

PBS: Africans in America: Nat Turner's Rebellion, 1831
http://www.pbs.org/wgbh/aia/part3/3p1518.htm.

GLOSSARY

betray (bee-TRAY)—To act in a way that is not loyal or faithful to
someone.

conductor (kun-DUK-ter)—The person who operates a train.

disguises (dis-GUY-ses)—To change or hide the looks of.

plantation (plan-TAY-shun)—A large farm.

pneumonia (noo-MOHN-yuh)—A serious disease of the lungs.

punishment (PUH-nish-ment)—A consequence for doing
something wrong.

INDEX

Knifed Watercolors®

Marian Christy

goff BOOKS

Published by Goff Books, an Imprint of ORO Editions.

Executive publisher: Gordon Goff.

www.goffbooks.com

info@goffbooks.com

Graphic Design: Brooke Biro

Text and Images: Marian Christy

Goff Books Project Coordinator: Kirby Anderson

10 9 8 7 6 5 4 3 2 1 First Edition

Library of Congress data available upon request. World Rights: available.

ISBN: 978-1-943532-58-2

Color separations and printing: ORO Group Ltd.

Printed in China.

International distribution: www.goffbooks.com/distribution

ORO Editions makes a continuous effort to minimize the overall carbon footprint of its publications. As part of this goal, ORO Editions, in association with Global ReLeaf, arranges to plant trees to replace those used in the manufacturing of the paper produced for its books. Global ReLeaf is an international campaign run by American Forests, one of the world's oldest nonprofit conservation organizations. Global ReLeaf is American Forests' education and action program that helps individuals, organizations, agencies, and corporations improve the local and global environment by planting and caring for trees.

Knifed Watercolors®

Marian Christy

Marian Christy, inventor of *Knifed Watercolors®*, is a retired *Boston Globe* editor-columnist-writer who was nominated twice for The Pulitzer Prize (1983 and 1984). She is the only three-time winner of the prestigious J.C.Penney-University of Missouri Journalism Award (1966-1968-1970).

During her 26-year *Globe* career, she won 30 prizes for her newspaper. She has written four books on journalism, now ancillary reading by college students, and has contributed to the *New York Times Syndicate* and *Harper's Bazaar*. She is completing a fictional book about emotional abuse on the home front.

She won the international Cavaliere Medal from the Presidente Della Republica for her reporting of Italian fashion in Rome (1972). *Cosmopolitan Magazine* named her one of America's top five journalists (1978).

Franklin Pierce College (Rindge, New Hampshire) conferred on her an Honorary Degree, Doctor of Letters, (1987). Christy's papers are collected at Boston University's Howard Gotlieb Archival Research Center. She attended evening classes at Boston University while working full time and earned a Certificate in Journalism (1956). The University named her a Distinguished Alumni (1985).

While off-duty from painting newspaper stories, she had always secretly pursued her life's dream of painting brushed watercolors. It was in her inconsequential basement "studio," in one powerful flash, that she discovered that watercolors and palette knives belong together. This is her story.

One

I already knew that poorness and painting isn't a good match.

I already knew, but could not accept, Daddy's unbreakable law about women—even pretty ones—that they should never be heard or, worse, *heard from* in a public way.

And there I was, barely seventeen, living on pennies and dreaming big about building a creative career for myself. I've never labeled myself courageous. But I ventured to stand before my father, an immovable object, asking him to concede to me, a would-be irresistible force.

I beseeched this extreme chauvinist, the first man I'd ever known, to allow me to attend an affordable college that focused on painting and writing. His wallet would be unscathed. I'd do it on my own. I asked him to let me be me.

I spoke quietly, an octave above a whisper. He heard a lioness' roar: "I'll work for a year after I graduate from high school," I had pleaded. "It won't cost you anything. I'll pay my own way." Daddy stiffened. He became a human icicle wearing a dapper business suit with all the right accessories. His condescension was mighty. Obviously I was not a gambler on a roll.

My Name is White Eagle

His stabbing retort, with its toll of finality, was short and sour. "Ha-ha!" he laughed sarcastically.

A cloud of gloom descended into the space that divided us. It never went away. "Please!" I'd added stupidly, an afterthought, while surrendering my cherished hopes. I sounded exactly like the pitiful beggar I was. To underline his censure, Daddy turned his back on me and stomped out of the room. His condemnation was the end of it and me and painting and writing and college.

I'd just been emotionally demolished. I sobbed without making a sound.

I've always pictured my father's sarcastic "Ha-ha!" response as an exclamation point shaped like a sharp *knife*. His chuckle of contempt was buoyed by the cruelty of absolute male authority. It was as if I, and my self-vision, was non-existent at that crucial moment and probably forever.

I was a starved pre-Feminist then, a young go-getter without a reliable map. There were masses of emotionally wounded women like me everywhere, unknowns who wanted to make their own way.

They were clueless. They ran scared. So did I.

The fear of absolute daddy dictatorship controlling my creativity became shackled to my other primary fear.

I already knew that the artistic world is studded with painful rejections. I learned that at the library, scouring biographies of the bullied Impressionists who blazed trails and, like me, were laughed at.

I wondered how I could possibly be creative when potential critical reactions, rendered automatically and with a maddening carelessness, were an endless stream of disinterested no-nos.

Tough Sailing

Oh Happy Day

Shadows

Mars

Knifed Watercolors®

In Wonderland

Surging

How to Navigate

Two

I remember how I forced myself to look down at my worn-out penny loafers, shined but without coin, to avoid Daddy's eyes frozen with disapproval.

Still it was in this contentious context that I made my case.

He did not want his firstborn to be a daughter who was standing before him, shaking, and imploring his permission to be allowed to be a creative, to study art and writing in an inconsequential college that didn't cost too much.

I remember how my soft voice trembled with an inaudible clash of twin emotions: a clinging fear of my father's alpha power and a deep, deep longing to express myself creatively somehow.

I was squashed between a rock and a hard place.

Lost on the Prairie

Gardening

Three

But even Daddy, a classic sexist, could not put out the creative fire raging inside me. That longing has never been extinguished. It will exist as long as I do. I'm a Scorpio. According to astrological legend, I rise from my own ashes. I didn't consider occult predictions then. All I cared about was figuring out how to get from where I was, which was nowhere, to where I wanted to be.

I forgot about the power of kismet.

Destiny is notoriously fickle and totally unpredictable. You never know when fate will swoop in and take over. It may be tomorrow or take many tomorrows. When it moves in your favor, it can jet you to upper levels of worlds you never knew existed. You become a version of the Phoenix rising straight out of Greek mythology.

That's what happened to me. I learned a life lesson. Destiny, the ultimate rescuer, is more powerful than a prejudiced father forbidding female indulgence in anything artsy.

Runs Deep

Swamped

Four

One day, a million years after this old patriarchal collision, I was at my easel painting watercolors the classic way, with brushes.

I'd fiddled the day away. I assessed my work. It was not up to par. I had wasted time and art materials. I was angry with myself. I've always hated failure, even temporary failure.

Staring critically at the landscape that didn't excite me, I reached blindly for a big fat brush to paint a crisscross "x" from corner to corner of the image. That painting was about to be trashed. But not before I'd x'd it out and tore it up real good.

There was an "x" there all right, some sort of inexplicable hybrid graffiti.

Summer

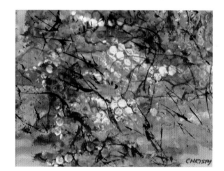

Winter

Ketching

Magnificent

Knifed Watercolors®

Rippling Along

The Blues

Good Morning

Bursting

Neptunian

Burbling

Reflections

Jagged Edges

Underneath the "x" was a gorgeous squiggle of colors blurring into each other. Watery shapes took forms on their own volition, without me.

How did this bizarre magic happen?

I glanced at my right hand. It clutched an old palette knife, a junky tool from the past, something I'd used to experiment with oils.

I stared, mesmerized, enchanted, and hypnotized by the "x."

This was a rare ah-ah moment, *ha-ha spelled backwards,* and its sudden melodrama illuminated my imagination, thundered into my soul and jolted my thinking.

I understood instantly that this was a supernatural message, an inspiration, an esoteric gift, something golden that I was destined to interpret or translate.

"What if?" I thought. What if I could figure out how to create whole watercolor paintings with palette knives? Was that even a possibility? Could I ditch brushes and paint landscapes, seascapes, and still lifes armed only with a puddle, watercolors and palette knives, no drawing?

The flickering fire that Daddy tried to extinguish years earlier suddenly exploded into an inferno.

Every working day for a decade-plus I toyed with the unlikely idea, played it out at my easel. I played and played and played. Mistakes, some were sloppy, showed me what not to do.

Finding My Way

Night the Moon Fell on Me

Five

I am a self-taught artist.

That means I have no pre-conceived notions. I know nothing about sticking to rules. I played the palette knives my way, independently. Sooner, rather than later, the "knifed watercolors," that's what I called them, took on a life of their own.

They assumed depths and dimensions unknown to watercolors.

If you touch the water in a knifed marine painting, you can feel the waves roll and break.

If you press your finger gently on the raised rocks in an image, they exude a rough, hard, impenetrable texture.

Knifed flowers appear silky but they seem to be reaching out beyond the paper.

I began to believe that this was the pioneering style I was born to paint. I envisioned my work as a 21st-century interpretation of modern watercolors: new and original, contemporary and unique. I still cannot fathom what strange force put that palette knife in my painting hand. All I know is that some ghostly presence had metamorphosed me into the inventor of a strikingly avant-garde watercolor style.

It turned out that no one thought I'd achieved anything but me.

Answered Prayers – Her

Your Majesty – His

Two years of trying to convince the militant attorneys at the United States Trademark Office that I had worked a minor miracle at an insignificant easel in my basement brought me genres of Daddy's ha-ha in legalese.

They were not impressed. No such painting style could be viable. This was the essence of a small pile of pompous rejections. But a soul on fire can become unstoppable.

Faces in the Crowd

Bar Hopping

Growing Up

Pooling of Ideas

Vibrancy

Industrial

Following the Golden Rule

Knifed Watercolors®

Windy

Six

I kept on watercolor painting with my knives. I was on a spectacular rollercoaster ride. The images became more sophisticated, more eye-catching, more appealing, and much more mysterious.

The palette knives talked to me and for me.

I used knives in all shapes and sizes. They became extensions of my hand. We merged our faculties. There were times when I actually thought that the palette knives moved my hand, told me what to do versus vice-versa.

Slowly I developed a palpable faith in my work. It became a metaphor of me, an unknown trailblazer working in the dark and craving to be seen in the light.

That's what prompted me to enter all kinds of computer-generated regional and national competitions. I won some. I lost some. Ultimately what I realized was a really good resume, proof on paper that knifed watercolors really existed.

In 2014 the Trademark Office was satisfied that I'd made a consequential inroad into the art world. My knifed watercolors became Knifed Watercolors®.

That weird mischance and perfect timing of picking up the wrong instrument, a discarded palette knife, became my big chance.

He Sent Me White Roses

Seven

My images are often studded with symbolic blockage that refers not only to my art journey but also to my life's journey.

I know all about obstruction.

There were times when I thought the Universe had passed me by, that I'd never be who or what I wanted to be. I thought that artistic conundrums, complicated ones, were my irrevocable fate.

When I told my late Mom, Anna, that it was true that nice guys finish last, she countered: "Nice guys finish at last."

It has taken me time to realize that destiny has its own time frame. It has nothing to do with calendars or clocks. My palette knives and I are, at last, in perfect tandem. It took us twelve years of practice to get in sync.

Rejection

Eight

The only art classes I've ever attended were two or three insignificant ones taught in high school.

They were tagged "elective" which meant that the art courses didn't count much in terms of an academic curriculum, just like I didn't count at home.

Those "trivial" classes, how I loved them, were the seeds of me as I am now: an accomplished artist against all odds. As I write this, I am in my 86th year.

I know what self-taught really means. That's truly what and who I am.

The first ploy I mastered is to let no one do your thinking for you. Your best weapon, aside from your painting tools, is to keep an open mind. Ideas come from nowhere and everywhere. Artists are, or should be, as absorbent as sponges.

Boldness is also a definite asset. Be bold.

Some artists think being nervy is better. That works too.

Reaching

Cold Courage

Eternity

Waiting 1

Waiting 2

Gnarled

Knifed Watercolors®

Happy Place

Nine

Pablo Picasso's illegitimate daughter, Paloma, then a seventeen-year-old amateur illustrator, tracked me down at The Meurice, a prestigious Paris hotel. All I knew then was that Paloma, whoever she was, had left with the concierge some very crude hastily inked fashion sketches signed only with her first name. Obviously this stranger didn't attend an art college either. When I gazed aghast at the rawness of her work, the concierge interrupted my stunned reaction. "Papa is Picasso," he said forcefully.

French law stipulated that since she was a love child, she had no access to the Picasso surname. I didn't know any of this as I fingered her bungled artwork.

Finally the concierge relayed Paloma's full message that sounded more like a demand rather than a polite petition. She wanted her untidy work featured in my newspaper.

Paloma's 1971 bold beg had punch. It was imaginative and brash.

It made me painfully aware that my 1950 Daddy beg had been too humble, too weak. I admired her chutzpah. She was a daredevil. I, at seventeen, had been merely a deferential darer. I was so flustered, so panicked by Daddy's laugh of doom, that I was unable to make eye contact with him.

Then a troubling thought hit me, the journalist.

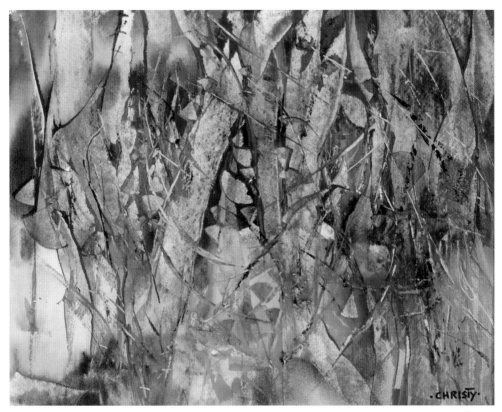

Charm

Pushy Paloma might be a fake. Maybe the concierge had been bribed. Quick research indicated that she had a burgeoning connection to designer Yves Saint Laurent.

I telephoned Saint Laurent's office. She was the real thing.

I invited her to lunch at The Meurice bar that happened to be in the shadow of the Louvre where Papa Picasso was the first living artist to be shown in its holy halls.

Two things stand out in that Paloma memory: Her nails were bitten to the quick just like mine were when I was seventeen. And I recall her telling me that if she tried to visit her father, he'd instructed a servant to tell her he wasn't home, to shoo her from his door. Impulsively Paloma had glanced *up* and there, staring down at her from an upstairs window was Papa, a tyrant who hated women artists no matter who they were. Paloma didn't tell me how much it hurt to be an art-prone daughter being cast off by her father. It was written in her eyes.

An eerie parallel was scrolled between us. We, two artistic teenagers, both had fathers who dismissed us brashly.

I understood perfectly the roots of Paloma's aggression. Getting her amateurish fashion illustrations published was something she had to do. Her presence was flamboyant. But her outward rakishness didn't disguise an inner hunger to be accepted and validated, if not by Papa, then by the outside world.

I arranged to have her naive sketches redone professionally and printed with my interview.

Power of Self

Technicolor

Fences

Splash

An Open Door

Sweltering

Splendor

Pristine Power

Huddling for Warmth

Asian Mystery

Beckoning

Knifed Watercolors®

Pandemonium

After she'd established herself as a Tiffany superstar, she'd telephone me now and then to talk fashion and art. In our last encounter in 1988, at Boston's Ritz- Carlton, she was the antithesis of her teenage self.

French laws had changed. She had use of her full name, Paloma Picasso, and she was an international celebrity and purveyor of luxury goods. She'd reportedly inherited $20 million from her father's estate and, best of all, a valuable collection of Picasso paintings. She refused to disclose how many.

According to 2018 news reports, one of Papa's paintings was auctioned for $106.5 million. Some reports go as high as $115 million.

It was at our final meeting that I realized Paloma's truth.

She was never haunted, compelled or consumed by the irresistible call of the easel. She had no interest in following in her father's footsteps. Maybe his shoes were too big. Her initial sketches, the ones she'd delivered to me in Paris, were a taboo subject. She'd forgotten that once, long ago, she'd been simply Paloma, eager hawker of her early illustrations.

All she wanted to talk about then was Paloma Picasso perfume, $120 an ounce.

Glorious

Ten

I apprenticed in Europe's snootiest fashion salons, not art school. I was totally unaware I was apprenticing. Something telepathic happened to me, something totally subconscious. I think of it as my subliminal miracle. I soaked it all up without knowing I was soaking it all up.

It was within the sacred confines of the European couture houses that theories about my future artistic adventures were being stimulated in the deepest terrain of my brain.

The effect was serious and indelible, like an unforgettable lecture by a fine professor that I'd recorded.

I discovered, up-close, how dauntless top designers were, how they hyperbolized colors and lines, how they manipulated shapes fearlessly, even ridiculously. I saw how they mesmerized, or ambushed, critical viewers into lusting for whatever they happened to create.

How was this trickery achieved? Was there some sort of secret formula? Then it hit me.

It all boiled down to the surprise element, the shock appeal and a bombshell charisma that was revelatory. A viewer reacts emotionally to runway shockers. That's a painter's focus too: to entice, to thrill, to generate curiosity. I scribbled these phenomena in my notes. I was there primarily as a fashion editor for a top American newspaper. But I couldn't help noticing that fashion is an art and that art is always in fashion. I willed myself to be unbiased, to open up to any wild idea that popped into my head.

Beginning to Break

Zooming Downhill

Solitude

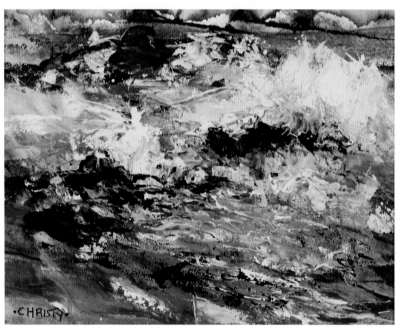

Getting Rough

A Sunflower is Born

Cherry Blossom Time

Golden Day

Complications

The Mall 1

Knifed Watercolors®

Christmas Shopping

Changing Wardrobes

Intense

Going for the Gold

Electricity

Eleven

The astonishing fashions that mannequins paraded by me exuded amazing creative confidence. Designers smashed enthralling palettes together, juxtaposing one against each other, and came up with unexpected eye-openers.

I was blown over by how audaciously their designs were executed and how authoritative they were even when the fashions were foolish. Defiance was written all over the Collections. I thought of designers as "the resistance," creators who were determined to change the norms.

I thought the prevalent sassiness in the couture world could revert to my paintings.

I cross-examined the collateral thoughts dancing in my brain.

Why are lips painted black and dubbed chic? Why do women swoon over t-shirts hemmed with lingerie lace? Why does a customer pay $725 for a plain Louboutin pump just because it has a red sole?

How could I apply this audacity to my knifed paintings? Why shouldn't a tree trunk be blue? Why can't a sky be green? Why can't autumn leaves be the color of lilacs? These unorthodox ideas prodded me, punched me, to be spunky enough to play outside the box.

Tulips on Blue

The fiercest couturiers, like their counterpart artists, have always sought to be innovators.

They avoided copying each other. Their autograph was their autograph. They established their individuality and never waivered.

Anyone who deigned to mimic them was dubbed a copycat. Collectively they thought what serious artists have always thought. A painted image should stand on its own merit, no further explanation necessary. There is no spoken commentary or blaring background music in European haute couture. It's all about the visual impact and what the viewer makes of it. A fascinating painting should have a similar set of dynamics. If you attend a gallery show, nobody explains in detail the artist's motive, method, or style. What you deduce is based on what you see and how it makes you feel inside.

After I filed my stories and satisfied my editors, I wrote extensive notes to myself, notes about fundamental moods and nuances that link fashion and art.

The notes, based on impromptu hunches and intuition, are tattooed on my spirit.

I was born with a desperate desire to push boundaries and blaze new trails. I needed to produce memorable art, something that would be mine alone.

These simmering desires, the ones that survived Daddy's rebuff, jabbed at me while I was watching mannequins sashay seductively down couturier runways.

If birds can fly, what can't I?

Finale

Falling in Love

Textured

Vibrations

Mystical Journey

Knifed Watercolors®

The Melt

Streaming

Knifed Watercolors®

My Hangout

A New Path

Solitary Flight

Go with the Flow

Knifed Watercolors®

Burnt Out

Twelve

I sign my Knifed Watercolors® with just my last name, my father's last name. You might think that's odd. Daddy was, after all, my first major rejecter.

If he hadn't laughed so tauntingly and further ignored me by walking away, I'd have told him what was in my heart. I wanted to tell Daddy that someday I'd make him proud that I had a God-given ability to sign his name to my marquee.

In deference to the millions of punctuating periods and hyphens I've used over a 26-year journalism career, I also put a dot, an inconsequential period, or even a whimsical dash, at each end of my one-name signature. Writing, and more writing, is what always kept my dream of painting afloat. It's how I paid for my painting supplies and exhibit fees.

All the years I honored tight deadlines, I painted while off-deadline. No one remarked that I'd never surrendered my first art dream. They just noticed that I wasn't around much. I had no friends. I wasn't a partygoer. I was somewhere alone, painting with brushes, a long prelude to painting watercolors a different way.

The dots I use, the imitation periods, are also a disguised deference to the points natural to palette knives.

I like points.

I like making my point. I like people to get my point. That's what fashion designers do. That's what artists do.

The Mall 2

Daddy never knew about my being in Paris, Rome, London, Dublin, Athens, and Madrid to cover Haute Couture shows in an era when the fashion world was still at its most glorious peak of respect.

He never knew that I skipped formal lunches to sit at a sidewalk café with my sketchbook, drawing scenes, quick portrayals of street landscapes that I'd later paint at home.

I wish I could have told him how the couture world, the one in which I starred journalistically, had been my primitive artistic beacon, the one that kept my incessant urge to paint intact.

I wish that I could have shown him that I didn't need formal training. Daddy died before I became a successful writer still determined to be a successful, even triumphant, painter.

Looking Down

The universe had picked me up and plucked me down in the best inner sanctums of world-class designers who were artists using a medium different from mine.

It was at these far-flung places, watching runways become an ostentatious stage for clothes that boggled the imagination, that I picked up on the esoteric basics of what it means to be an inspired creative.

I wish I could have told him that after our heartbreaking confrontation, I had painted regularly in secret. I had hidden my first primitive watercolors and scribbles in a locked metal box under my bed.

Daddy shunned me. He wanted nothing to do with a budding female artist. My work was safe. He bypassed my little room. The teenage paintings, the ones I'd hid, now hang on walls that surround me. I'm looking at them while I tell you my zigzag story. I still think of Daddy's laughter as the ironic thrust of a *knife*. Sometimes, when I'm caught between wide-awakeness and sleep, when I'm in some sort of otherworldly reverie, I think about the varied significances of knives.

The Tempest

Crashing

Flying High

Instant Attraction

Ghosts Emerging

Unexpected

Disorientation

Getting Emotional

Dancing Trees

Thirteen

When a baby is born in rural areas of Third World countries, a fishing knife may be the only way to cut the cord. Knives, then, are linked to new beginnings.

Many of my knifed landscape paintings have open spaces meant to signify an opening up. These are my esoteric symbols of unforeseen opportunity.

The knife symbolizes the cuts in life, the gashes and tears that break your heart. No one escapes these wounds.

A knife can also be like the legendary Damocles sword hanging over your head. There's a storm brewing. Beware. Squalls and tempests in my marine paintings contain that communiqué.

It's with a knife that you get to the core of things in the kitchen.

I am not a plein-air artist. I work indoors, downstairs, in a humble corner I dub my "studio."

When I want the truth to be revealed in a painting, I cut away the extraneous with my palette knives. They help me figure out what to eliminate, what to leave in.

The Still Waters

Fourteen

When I was four years old, I discovered a tattered old encyclopedia open on the floor. I sat down in front of it, amazed. I pointed to a "picture," a black and white illustration that helped define a word.

My mother told me that I said, "me!" as if I meant it.

Roots

I See the Light

Fifteen

The first turndown that preceded my father's "ha-ha" reaction happened in the fourth grade, in a private parochial school under the aegis of Sister Lucien. We were told to draw and paint an orange, the fruit, a circle in one color only: orange. We were told precisely how an orange is drawn. It was chalked on the board. Deviation was not acceptable. Sister made that clear.

"Do not digress," she warned. "Do exactly as you're told." My orange painting shattered Sister Lucien's rule of conformity. I outlined the fruit in black and gave it a matching stem. It looked prettier that way. I knew nothing then of Van Gogh's "Starry Night" painting or that the village buildings were outlined in black.

As Sister Lucien collected the paintings she promised that everyone's work would be displayed on the walls of the class.

The next day I arrived early in class to view the Orange Exhibit. My drawing, only mine, was missing.

Gogh Country

Quagmire

Bye Bye Blackbird

Knifed Watercolors®

Cheers

Pussy Willows

Like an Elephant

Green

Rocky

Knifed Watercolors®

Teeming

Uprising

Sister Lucien found me despairing at my desk, my face buried in the arms that lay on top of the desk. I didn't have to explain why.

"It's because you did what you wanted to do," she chided. There was a sharp edge in her voice. "That's called disobedience." She floated away huffily, her headdress fluttering around her shoulders.

I'm glad she didn't thrash my fingers with her wooden ruler. Instead she aroused my mutiny. I know that's the exact moment that I took a vow to stick to originality no matter what. I was in the embryo stage of rebellion.

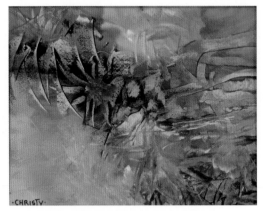

Jellyfish Sting

Mystery of the Night

Sixteen

My artistic ambitions have never been vague. They never fell into the "want" category. This was what my future had to contain. I had to paint stories. I had to write stories. I had to be artistic or die trying. Creative desires ran so deep within the rivers of me they became, and still are, my controllers, my magnificent obsession. What's strange, and moving, is that in some perverse way, everything and everyone that I've told you about here represents the signposts that led me on my long and circuitous journey to Knifed Watercolors®.

Pride and Prejudice

Vernal Equinox